# Stories
## of the Saints

Margaret McAllister

ILLUSTRATED BY
Alida Massari

LION
CHILDREN'S

*For my Mytholmroyd friends   M.M.*
*To my little friends Diana, Giulia, and Roberta   A.M.*

Text copyright © 2015 Margaret McAllister
Illustrations copyright © 2015 Alida Massari
This edition copyright © 2015 Lion Hudson

The right of Margaret McAllister to be identified as the author and of Alida Massari to be identified as the illustrator of this work has been asserted by them in accordance with the Copyright, Designs and Patents Act 1988.

Published by Lion Children's Books
an imprint of
**Lion Hudson plc**
Wilkinson House, Jordan Hill Road,
Oxford OX2 8DR, England
www.lionhudson.com/lionchildrens

ISBN 978 0 7459 6445 4

First edition 2015

A catalogue record for this book is available from the British Library

Printed and bound in Malaysia, October 2014, LH18

# Contents

# Saint Peter

I USED TO SAY that the greatest thing about our Peter was his feet. When you think about the size of Peter's feet, you wonder how he managed to get them in his mouth so much. If ever a man could put both feet in it at once, it was our Peter. Mind you, he had plenty of practice.

When Peter first met Jesus, it could have been a catastrophe. It very nearly was. Peter — he was called Simon in those days, but I always think of him as Peter now — Peter and the lads had been fishing all night and not caught a thing… not a sardine. They'd had a long night. Then Jesus turned up, stood there on the shore, and told them to row back out again and fish on the other side of the boat.

Peter stood up very slowly with his face turning red. Everyone except Jesus took a step back. Even Peter's own brother Andrew didn't tell Peter how to fish. What chance did Jesus, the carpenter, have?

"All right, if you say so," said Peter without a smile. "If you say so, we'll row out on the lake and cast out the nets."

You could tell what would happen next. If they came back this time without any fish, the next thing going in the lake would be Jesus. Head first.

And then, before we
know it, what a commotion
there was as they rowed back
to shore! That little boat was
rocking low in the water with the
weight of fish; they had to wave
James and John over to help them and share
the load. Everyone cheered — we couldn't help it! We'd never
seen such a catch. Peter jumped out of the boat and fell to his knees
at Jesus' feet.

You'd think he would have said, "Thank you." He didn't. He said,
"Go away, Lord.

"Go away. You're from God — you're not like the rest of us. I'm a
sinful man, I'm rough and ready — all I know is this place, and the fishing,
and my family. I shouldn't be in the company of a holy man like you, sir."

Jesus sorted that one out. He invited Peter to become one of his team.
I suppose he could have said no. But he didn't.

Peter never did things by halves. After that, wherever Jesus went, Peter was with him. Even when Jesus walked on water, Peter got out of the boat to walk to him – well, to be honest, he fell in. He stopped looking at Jesus and looked at his own big feet instead, realizing that there was no way they could stay afloat. It's a good thing Jesus grabbed him.

Seriously, there was a time when Jesus stood in dazzling white on a mountaintop and Peter swears he saw Moses and Elijah up there with him. And what did Peter do? Open his big mouth and offer to put up tents for them. Bless him.

He put his feet in it again when Jesus said he had to go to Jerusalem and be crucified, but it was only because he couldn't bear the thought of that happening to Jesus. So he said, "No, Lord, that won't happen to you." Jesus put him right about that. But he still left Peter in charge. That's where the name "Peter" came from, because it means "rock".

"You are Peter the Rock," said Jesus. "I'm going to build my church on this rock."

There was one time when Peter wasn't at Jesus' side. Poor Peter; he didn't manage to be a rock when Jesus was taken away by the soldiers. They took Jesus to the high priest's house, and Peter had the courage to follow him that far, I'll say that much for him. But when the servants noticed him, and started asking him questions about whether he was anything to do with Jesus, Peter swore he'd never seen him in his life. Before the cock crowed and the sun rose, he had disowned Jesus three times.

He knew what was coming to Jesus. You can't blame him for being scared. What would you have done? Then they brought Jesus out; he looked at Peter, and Peter went away and sobbed his heart out.

When Jesus came back from the dead, it was a new start for Peter. The bit with the boat and all the fish happened again, and then Jesus asked Peter, "Do you love me?" Three times he asked it, and this time, Peter said yes every time.

And he meant it. He led worship, he taught about Jesus, he healed, and yes, he still put his foot in it. He wouldn't stop talking about Jesus, and that got him put into prison, but he never let down Jesus' people, or the poor, or the needy. He still made mistakes, but I think that's why we loved him.

Peter. Big feet. Great heart.

*Peter the fisherman was one of the three disciples closest to Jesus (the others were James and John).*
*He became the leader of the young Church and was crucified in about 64 CE.*

# Saint Paul

WHEN I RODE out this morning, I had a purpose. I had a place to go and work to do – brutal work, but it had to be done. Now, I'm in the dark. I'm in a strange place, everyone speaks in whispers, and I'm as blind and helpless as a kitten. I need people to bring me food and wine and guide me to bed. Dear God, what is happening? Where are you?

I am an Israelite, one of God's chosen people, and I love studying the Scripture. The excellent Rabbi Gamaliel was my teacher. When Jesus of Nazareth turned up from the north with his raggle-taggle of followers who knew more about fish than faith, I thought, "Here's another one. In his own village they probably think he's wonderful. In Jerusalem he's just another nuisance."

I was glad when they killed him. What did he expect? As far as the crowd was concerned, any man who rides a donkey into Jerusalem with everyone singing "Hosanna" is sent by God. He virtually said he *was* God. There's only one way after that and it's death, but before a week was out his followers were saying he was back again. Larger than life.

They were calling him messiah, Son of God; they claimed to be working miracles in his name. It was dangerous madness, and had to be stopped.

Somebody had to do it. I had "The Followers of the Way" arrested and thrown into prison. In Jerusalem, I had them killed. I never threw the stones myself, but I held the coats for the men who did. The Followers got the message. They ran away. Some of them went to Damascus, so I got permission to follow them there and sort them out. That's where I was going this morning.

I was riding to Damascus with a couple of assistants following me when the light came. Try to imagine lightning, but not in the sky; imagine lightning striking right in front of you, and through you, too. The power and the shock made my horse rear up and throw me to the ground, and I swear to you, truly and honestly, I heard a voice that called:

"Saul! Why are you persecuting me?"

I didn't know that voice and in the dazzling light I could see nobody, but that voice was powerful, and I had to respect it. "Who are you, Lord?" I cried.

"I am Jesus, the one you are persecuting," said the voice. "Now, go on to Damascus. Wait there. Only wait."

As I picked myself up from the ground, I waited for my sight to come back to normal. And then slowly, with a churning of fear, I realized that it was not coming back to me. The light had left me blind.

The men who were with me had seen the light from a distance, but they had no idea what I was talking about when I said somebody had spoken to me. I was no longer the man in command, riding in front. I had to be put on my horse and led like a child.

It's been three days. I don't want the food they bring me. I wait, as the voice told me to. What else can I do?

Somebody opens a door. "Are you Saul?" says a voice.

This is not the voice that spoke to me on the road. It's the voice of an ordinary man.

"Saul?" he says again, and his voice comes nearer until I can reach out and touch him.

"Yes, I'm Saul," I say.

"Good," he says. "Good. My name is Ananias, and I'm a follower of Jesus. I was praying, and I heard the voice of Jesus telling me to come to Straight Street and find a man called Saul. Do you understand? He sent me to you."

I remember the voice on the road. *I am Jesus, the one you are persecuting.* A terrible thought is forming in my head. Jesus truly is from God. I have led the fight against his people, and now I must answer for it. Blind and helpless, I must answer to God for what I have done.

"Why has he sent you?" I ask.

"To call you to serve him," he said. "He has chosen you, Saul. He requires me to pray for you to receive the Holy Spirit, and be well."

He lays his hands on my head and suddenly I remember that bright flash of lightning. Then I feel something falling from my eyes, as if my sight is set free. I see an honest man, his eyes closed in prayer. I see reality. I see a future with Jesus.

*After his Damascus Road experience, Saul changed his name to Paul and became an ardent Christian. He journeyed widely, starting new churches and moving on, and his letters to these churches are in the New Testament. He was convinced that the gospel of Jesus Christ was for everyone and that we can be united to God by the life, death, and resurrection of Jesus Christ.*

# Saints Perpetua and Felicity

AFTER PERPETUA'S BABY had been taken away from her, she decided that nothing worse could happen. She knew her family would look after her little boy, so he'd be safe and well. But even if she was thrown to the wild beasts – which she probably would be – nothing could be worse than parting from her baby.

It was the year 203 CE and Perpetua was recently widowed with a baby son and living in Carthage, a part of North Africa governed by Rome. Under Roman rule everybody had to worship the emperor and Perpetua refused to do that, so she had been thrown into a deep, dark prison cell. Her friend Felicity was with her – Felicity, who was expecting a baby very soon, was Perpetua's slave girl, but they were friends, too. Four Christian men were in prison with them.

Perpetua's father had begged her to give up her faith. He argued with her for days, and finally she pointed to a water jar.

"What's that?" she asked.

"It's a jar, of course," said her father.

"Exactly," said Perpetua. "It's a jar, it just is, and it can't be anything else. I'm a Christian, I just am, and I can't be anything else."

So Perpetua and her friends were taken to prison and told that they would be put to death by being thrown to wild beasts in the arena. They went on praying, praising God and encouraging each other, and some of their friends paid the guards to give them a more comfortable room in the prison. They weren't afraid of dying, but Perpetua found Felicity crying one day.

"Felicity, they won't put you to death," said Perpetua. "They never kill a pregnant woman, because that would be killing the innocent baby, too."

"But my baby isn't due yet," wept Felicity. "By the time it's born you will have been killed, and I'll have to face it all alone."

But soon afterwards, Felicity gave birth to a baby girl, who was adopted by some Christian friends. Only days later, she and Perpetua were taken out to the arena to be put to death in front of the crowds. As they prayed, a wild heifer was sent to charge at them. It ran at Perpetua and threw her over its back on to the floor, but she calmly picked herself up and straightened her hairstyle, which had come loose. The heifer charged again, this time at both of them, and they helped each other to their feet.

The soldiers in charge of the arena were getting worried that if these two women continued as bravely as this, the crowd would soon be on their side. They allowed Perpetua and Felicity to exchange the kiss of peace, and then put them both to death quickly with a sword.

*Perpetua and Felicity bravely stood up to Perpetua's family as well as the Roman authorities by refusing to worship the emperor.*

# Saint Patrick

SOMETIMES A DAY comes that changes your life, and you don't see it coming. I got up that morning ready for an ordinary day, keeping an eye on my father's beasts, maybe, or studying if I felt like it. By nightfall, I was in the stinking hold of a slave ship.

We lived in West Britain and my parents had raised me to be a Christian, but I never really prayed until that day, when raiders came up the river grabbing anyone young and strong enough to be sold. Sold, yes, when I was sixteen. I was a slave in Ireland for six years herding animals with no other Christians anywhere near me, but that was where my faith grew. I turned to God because God was all I had to hold on to, and he never let me down. Jesus had never been so real to me as he was in those years of slavery.

After six years I escaped and somehow managed to get across the country and find a boat that would take me home, but I was restless. I wasn't the boy I'd been when I went away. I'd learned a lot about the world, about Ireland, about God, and about myself in those long rainy nights of prayer. I'd changed. The greatness and the goodness of Jesus Christ had become real for me, and I knew I had to go back to Ireland, taking the gospel with me.

I went to France to train as a priest first, then returned to Ireland. In my slavery years I'd learned the local language, so I could speak to the ordinary people in words they understood. They loved it, but not everybody there was pleased.

Ireland was governed by a king and the pagan priests, the Druids, who had far too much power. They ruled the people through fear. I taught the gospel of the Christ who brings freedom from evil, forgives sins, and pours out abundant life on all people, and they hated me for it. We were bound to clash. Before Easter I gathered a group of Christians together; we prayed, and set out for Slane. It was a sacred place for the Druids and a sacred time for us all.

The Druids were holding a festival. They gathered at the Hill of Tara and declared that all fires should be put out until the beacon was lit at the king's royal hall. They ordered a night of pitch darkness. But for Christians the night before Easter was a holy night, when the Easter fire must be kindled, so on the

Hill of Tara we lit the holy fire and watched as its warmth brightened the sky.

The Druids were enraged. They came out with their slaves and the king's men, swearing to find and kill us, but God was with us and protected us. Not one of us was harmed. The Druids reported afterwards that the only living thing they had seen on the hill was a deer, and the story went about that I had turned into a deer to avoid capture.

We prayed a prayer like this, and to this day it's called "The Deer's Cry":

*I bind the power of Christ to myself today,*
*Christ with me and within me,*
*Christ ahead of me and behind me, on either side of me, above me*
*   and below me,*
*To encourage and protect me.*
*Christ in calm and in danger.*
*Christ in everyone I meet today.*

Patrick was born in 387 CE, probably in south-west Scotland or
north-west England, and was captured and taken into slavery in Ireland at the
age of sixteen. After his escape he became a priest, then a bishop, and returned to
preach Christianity in Ireland. Following his challenge to the Druids at Tara, the king allowed
him to preach freely in Ireland. The Druids continued to threaten and harass Patrick and his companions,
but they still journeyed throughout the country, made converts, and established churches. Patrick
would spend weeks fasting and praying for Ireland. He died on 17 March 493.

# Saints Cyril and Methodius

THE YEAR WAS 862, and the emperor wanted someone to teach about Jesus Christ in the country of Moravia, where the Slav, or Slavonic, people lived. He appointed two brothers, Cyril and Methodius, and it turned out to be a very good choice.

The brothers were both priests, highly intelligent and extremely well educated, and they were both in important jobs. Methodius was a local governor and Cyril taught in a university, so they were both used to taking responsibility – and that wasn't all. They were both good at languages and spoke the Slavonic language fluently.

They went to Moravia and had a lot of success teaching about Jesus in the Slavonic tongue, but they felt uneasily that speaking wasn't enough. They needed to write things down. They wanted all the church services to be in a language the people understood, and for that they needed a written Slavonic language. At that time, everything that was written down in the Moravian church was in Greek and Latin, and a lot of the priests thought it should stay that way. Letting ordinary people understand the gospel was dangerous! There wasn't even an alphabet suitable to work with, so Cyril invented one based on the older Glagolitic script.

Cyril began work on a new written language, and after his death in 869 Methodius continued with his work. It wasn't always easy. Some people were jealous of his popularity, and there were always priests who thought that ordinary people shouldn't be able to read the Bible. For most of his life, Methodius faced opposition, and after his death in 885 there were still fierce arguments about writing things down in Slavonic. But today the alphabet Cyril invented is used widely in Eastern Europe, and is called "Cyrillic" after him.

*Brothers Cyril and Methodius are still remembered fondly for bringing the Gospels to the Slavs and founding their literature.*

# Saints Francis and Clare

FRANCESCO BERNARDONE WAS a young man with money and wanted to live life to the full. As the son of a rich cloth merchant, he had plenty of chances to do that. For Francis, "living life to the full" meant music, good clothes, and having a great time with his friends. He was fun and popular. He knew how to party.

He lived in Assisi, an Italian town. When fighting broke out between Assisi and the next town, Perugia, Francis chose the excitement of being a soldier, and rode into battle.

It wasn't so exciting when he was injured and taken prisoner, and remained in prison for nearly a year. But prison gave him thinking time, and praying time, too; after he was freed, his old way of life didn't appeal to him any more. He had planned to do more soldiering, but his heart was no longer in it. He was more interested in helping a leper than in galloping into battle. Back in Assisi, he went to the little chapel of St Damian to pray.

It was a neglected chapel, almost falling down. And it was the place where Francis heard God speaking to him.

"Francis," said the voice, "my church is falling into ruin. Build it for me."

At first Francis supposed that he had to rebuild the little chapel, and he sold his horse to pay for the work. Only God mattered to him now, and he wanted to live as Christ lived, serving the poor and needy. He gave away all he had and a lot of cloth from the family's warehouses, which enraged his father. His parents wanted him to settle down, get married, and stop giving away the family's merchandise, but Francis said that he had embraced "Lady Poverty". He owned nothing but the clothes he wore. At a monastery, he begged for work. Everything he got he shared with the poor, barely keeping enough to feed himself, yet he had a great joy in living. Lepers were believed to be so infectious that nobody would go near them, but Francis cared for them. Everywhere he went, he taught about Jesus. Other men came to join him, and the ministry of "the little poor man" began.

Not only men wanted to live the simple life. Clare, a young noblewoman, was eighteen and very beautiful, and had already received two proposals of marriage. She left home, cut off her hair, and asked to join Francis's order. It meant going hungry, sleeping on a hard bed, and shivering through the winter, but she threw herself into the life. Other wealthy young women joined them, including Clare's sister Agnes.

To Francis everything God had made was part of the same family. Sun, moon, stars and sky, earth, and water were brothers and sisters to Francis. He talked to animals and birds, and advised fish not to get caught.

One of Francis's companions once rescued a rabbit from a trap and, wondering what to do with it, brought it to Francis. It jumped straight into his lap and stayed there while he told it to be more careful in future and not get trapped. He put it down so it could run away, and it jumped back up again. The companion who'd brought it carried it to the shelter of the trees, but as soon as his back was turned the rabbit followed him back to Francis and climbed into his lap again. It had to be taken half a mile into the forest before it finally decided to stay away.

The people of Gubbio sent for Francis because they were terrified. A big hungry wolf had come to their little town, prowling for food. It preyed on farm animals and on people, too. They hardly dared to leave their houses, and no child was allowed to play outside. They huddled inside their homes and watched from the windows as Francis walked to the town.

The wolf had seen him, too. As Francis approached, it crouched, ready to spring. It had tasted human flesh already and wanted more. It tensed, snarled, and sprang for Francis's throat.

Francis raised one hand and made the sign of the cross. There must have been power in that gesture because the wolf stopped in mid-air and landed crouching at his feet.

"Brother Wolf!" said Francis. "This won't do!"

The wolf cowered before him.

"Brother Wolf," continued Francis. "What do you think you're doing, stealing from these good people? And eating people! Don't you know how bad that is? You were hungry. We all get hungry. But, Wolf! Eating people!"

The wolf lowered its head. It looked sorry.

"Now, Wolf," Francis went on kindly. "You did it because you were hungry, very hungry. I sometimes go for days without eating, too. So this is what I'll do. I'll tell these people to feed you and take care of you. On your

part, you must leave them in peace."

The wolf raised a paw to show that it understood.

"Good wolf," said Francis, and he walked to the town with the wolf following at his heels like a well-trained dog. The people crept from their houses, holding tightly to their children's hands while Francis explained that they must look after the wolf, and that the wolf had promised not to eat them. They kept their promise. So did the wolf, and in time Gubbio became very proud of it.

One of the remarkable facts about Francis is that the marks of the crucifixion showed on his hands and feet. During a night of prayer he had a vision of Christ in which these marks suddenly appeared, and he carried them for the rest of his life.

Francis asked Clare to begin a separate group for women. At first they were known as "The Poor Ladies" but later they became known as the "Poor Clares", and still are. To them, poverty was joyous freedom. But Clare herself was often ill, sometimes too ill to go to Mass. She didn't mind going without warm clothes and good food, but missing Mass was a hardship.

In a hut made of timber and plaster is a room with one tiny high window. It is dim even in daylight, and this is late on Christmas Eve. One candle shines a little light on a small bed with rough blankets. In the bed, Clare is propped up on pillows. She looks thin and pale. She passes her rosary beads through her fingers as she whispers her prayers and thinks of the old, beautiful story of the birth of Jesus. Her friend Francis will be telling that story at Mass that evening. He will even bring animals into the church and fill a manger with straw, so that people can feel that they are in the Bethlehem stable.

As she prays, a light begins to glow on the wall opposite. Pictures appear. She is looking at the church filled with people singing their Christmas hymns. Francis leads the animals into church. She can even see the wounds on his hands. When the singing is over, Francis tells that lovely story of Jesus Christ coming to earth as a helpless child for love of us all. The bread and wine are brought to the table. The people kneel.

Presently, a sister comes to her room. "I thought you might be lonely, Mother Clare," she says. "I know you wanted to go to Mass."

"God is good," says Clare in contentment. "I have all I need."

*Clare recovered and was with Francis at his death in October 1226, when he sang a welcome to "Sister Death". She died in 1253 at the age of sixty.*

# Saint Martin De Porres

I DON'T KNOW WHY they call me a saint. I was a misfit!

I was born in Lima, Peru, and lived there all my life. My father was a Spanish nobleman and my mother a local black woman, and it wasn't easy to be a mixed-race child in the late 1500s, especially after my father left us. Mixed-race children, such as my little sister Juana and I, were "mulattos" and could be sold as slaves. But God is good, and we remained free. I studied medicine, and later I gained my heart's dearest desire. In Lima there was an order of monks called the Dominican friars, and they let me join them.

Mulattos weren't allowed to take final vows as friars but I was happy as a lay brother, whether I was healing the sick, working in the kitchen, or kneeling in prayer. Later the prior, who was in charge, ignored the rules and let me take vows, so I was a professed Dominican brother – but I was still a mulatto, so when the order needed money to pay a debt, I suggested that they should sell me. They wouldn't! God is good!

I would have loved to be a missionary and travel the world, but somehow the world came to me. People of all classes and races arrived needing care and healing; so many! But God was at work and I was always able to find enough

food or beg enough money to help them. Somehow, God healed through my touch. Rich and poor, all races, they needed love and care. When a leper came to our monastery, how could I turn him away?

All God's creatures need care, including the animals. I could never bear to eat meat. Juana ran a hospice and also a hospital for cats and dogs, so they always had a place of safety.

Everybody likes me to tell the story about the mice. It was so simple! The mice had moved into the wardrobe where we kept sheets and clothing for the hospital. The brothers wanted to poison them, but it seemed to me that

the mice should have a home — just not in our wardrobe. I sat on the floor and explained to them that they really shouldn't eat poor people's sheets and clothes, and would they like me to find them a safe new home with plenty to eat? They seemed to think this was perfectly reasonable because they followed me down to the bottom of the garden and stayed there. I fed them every day and we never had any more problems with them. People were much more trouble than mice.

Some of the brothers said that a bright light appeared when I was praying, or even that I lifted up bodily from the ground. I wouldn't know about that. I only know that prayer was always a great blessing and joy to me. Living in God meant prayer and loving service. That was my life.

*Saint Martin de Porres was born in Lima in 1579 and died there in 1639. He was known for his care for all people and animals. Miracles of healing were connected with him, and he appears to have walked through walls to minister to people in a locked room.*

# Saint Teresa of Avila

Teresa wasn't afraid of a struggle. Just as well, because she had to face a lot of them.

She was born at Avila in Spain in 1515 to Don Alonso Sánchez de Cepeda and his wife Doña Beatriz. Don Alonso took his Christian faith very seriously and was a strict man who wouldn't allow novels in the house. Doña Beatriz was altogether different, a faithful Christian who liked her romantic novels and read them in secret. This didn't make life easy for Teresa when her father told her never to lie, and her mother told her to say nothing about the novels! Sometimes she felt that whatever she did, it would be wrong.

As a little girl she loved stories of saints who died heroically for their faith. She found this so inspiring that at five years old she persuaded her brother to run away with her to a non-Christian country "and beg them, for the love of God, to cut off our heads". They were beyond the city walls before their uncle saw them and brought them home.

When Teresa was fourteen her mother died, and Teresa, who missed her terribly, prayed to Mary the mother of Jesus to be her mother. Teresa became a teenager who liked a little gossip, fashion, and flirting as much as any girl, which

worried her father. He sent her to be educated at a convent.

By the time she was twenty, Teresa felt she had a choice to make: a traditional way of life like her mother's, or dedication to God in a convent. She felt that as long as she lived in the outside world she'd choose fun over God, and if she was ever to take her faith seriously she must choose the convent. Against her father's wishes, that was where she went.

She had hoped that in the convent there would be nothing to distract her from the life of prayer. She soon discovered that the Carmelite Covent of the Incarnation was more like a college for daughters of wealthy families. Nuns wore jewellery, entertained visitors, and flirted with any young men who were visiting. Teresa, who wanted to commit herself to prayer, found she couldn't concentrate. After a serious illness that left her mentally and physically exhausted she almost gave up praying altogether, but a priest encouraged her to persevere. She found that though she still sometimes found prayer hard, dull, and unrewarding, there were also times of great joy and inspiration. "The important thing is not to think much but to love much," she said, "and so do what encourages us to love. Love is not great delight but desire to please God in everything."

There were times when she had wonderful experiences in prayer, saw visions of Jesus, and felt she was at one with God. Sometimes she experienced "levitation", when the body lifts off the floor. She didn't like this to happen in public, and asked the nuns to sit on her so she couldn't float toward the ceiling! She referred to God as "Your Majesty".

By the age of forty-three Teresa was thoroughly tired of living in a convent that she found too comfortable, casual, and gossip-filled, so she planned to open a new convent with an emphasis on prayer and simplicity. Some of the sisters at the Convent of the Incarnation were angry. The people in the town were annoyed, too, and the leaders of the Catholic Church wondered what this awkward nun was up to, but finally she was allowed to open St Joseph's Convent "for the Discalced Carmelites". ("Discalced" means "without sandals".) By the time this was established her health was failing, but she journeyed with her nuns through Spain opening more convents on the same lines, through appalling weather and rough terrain. Often local people were wary and unwelcoming.

One on occasion, when she and her nuns were struggling on a long journey through a thunderstorm, soaked and exhausted, she shook her fist at heaven and cried, "Is this the way Your Majesty treats your friends?"

"Yes," was the answer. "I treat all my friends like this, Teresa."

"Well, no wonder you have so few of them!" she yelled.

In spite of all the opposition, young women were eager to join Teresa's order and people came to her to learn about prayer. But by 1582 her health had completely broken down and she died in October that year at the age of sixty-seven.

*Teresa of Avila is regarded as one of the Church's greatest teachers on prayer.*
*Here are some of her thoughts and prayers:*

Let nothing disturb you.
Let nothing make you afraid.
All things are passing.
God never changes.
Patience gains all things.
If you have God you will want for nothing.

God alone suffices.

Christ has no body now but yours,
No hands, no feet on earth but yours,
Yours are the eyes with which he looks with compassion on the world,
Christ has no body now on earth but yours.

# Saint Ignatius of Loyola

IGNATIUS HAD BIG plans for his life. God wasn't part of them.

He was born in 1491 in the town of Loyola in Spain, the youngest child in a noble Spanish family, and longed to be a soldier. The books he loved were stories about knights, and battles, and he couldn't wait to wear a sword. He wanted to be famous for his courage in war and rescue beautiful women who would fall in love with him. To his delight, when he was still young he was sent to the court of King Ferdinand and Queen Isabella. Soon he was a courtier and soldier and looked the part, wearing his cloak thrown back to show his sword and stylish boots. For years he lived the life he'd longed for, fighting duels and enjoying admiration.

By the age of thirty he was a brilliant soldier. When the Spanish town of Pamplona was attacked by the French, Ignatius fought to save it. Faced with a French army of twelve thousand men, the town surrendered. Ignatius didn't! He barricaded himself into the fortress with eighty soldiers and fought on, ready to die rather than surrender. He was still fighting when a cannon ball hit him in the legs and brought him down, with one leg shattered and the other badly injured.

The French were full of admiration for the man who had fought so
courageously. They took care of him and carried him on a litter back to the
castle at Loyola; surgeons were sent for, even though he was thought to be
dying.

Before the days of anaesthetics the setting of bones and stitching of wounds
must have been agony, but Ignatius was proud to say afterwards that he never
cried out, only clenching his fists against the pain. When the treatment was
over, he realized that one leg had an ugly bump where a bone was lying at an
angle. It looked wrong, and how could he get his best court stockings on over
that? He instructed the surgeons to break the bone again and reset it, and again
he bore it without flinching. It looked better, but he limped for the rest of his
life.

When the surgery was complete and he had come through a feverish illness
that followed it, Ignatius needed rest. There was nothing to do but read and
daydream.

"I'll read the books I enjoyed when I was a boy," he said. "*King Arthur and
His Knights*, *El Cid*, that sort of thing. Good stories with adventure and battles."

"There aren't any of those here," he was told. "We've only got stories of
Jesus and the saints."

Ignatius sighed and rolled his eyes. It would have to do. He spent the next few weeks reading the books he was given, and grew to love those stories.

He daydreamed, too. Sometimes he imagined riding to battle again, doing heroic deeds and winning the love of a beautiful noblewoman, but these daydreams left him bored. Then he imagined himself doing wonderful things for God. Saint Francis, for example, had given up everything for God. Ignatius came to admire him. "If that's what Francis did, what should I do?" He imagined giving up everything for God, and these daydreams inspired and encouraged him. By the time he was fully well, he had chosen Jesus Christ instead of the sword. He left his weapons before a shrine of the Virgin Mary, and became a priest, pilgrim, and teacher.

When he was unwell he had learned to turn his daydreams into prayer, and so to pray with his imagination. He soon realized that anyone could do it! This is one of the most valuable gifts he gave to the Church. "Use your imagination," he might say. "Imagine that you are there in a Gospel story with Jesus. What can you see, hear, touch, taste, and smell? What's happening? What do you say to Jesus? What does he say to you?"

*Ignatius of Loyola gave up everything to devote his life to God.*
*He founded an order of monks called the Society of Jesus,*
*or "Jesuits", and taught ways of praying, understanding,*
*and choosing that are still practised and valued today.*
*He died in 1556.*

# Saint Bernadette of Lourdes

BERNADETTE DOESN'T GO to school much. Since her father lost his job, the family have been so poor that they live in a squalid room with never quite enough to eat and not enough fuel to keep warm in the winters, short of everything except love. She gets asthma very badly, and she's often ill, which means she's missed so much school that she can't read and write. She can't even speak proper French, just her own local dialect. Some people say she's simple-minded. Stupid, slow Bernadette from the wrong side of town. Fourteen, and can't learn her lessons.

On a cold February day Bernadette, her sister Toinette, and their friend are out collecting firewood. The other girls are ahead and have waded across the river, but the cold air is making Bernadette's lungs hurt so she sits down near a cave opening that she calls "The Grotto". If she must cross the water, she'll do it further along where it's shallower. She's taking off her shoes and stockings when a gust of wind makes her look up.

In the opening of The Grotto is a rose bush, and from somewhere behind it comes a cloud of gold – then an astonishingly beautiful young lady! Bernadette stares. The Lady wears white, with a veil and a blue sash; there are roses at her feet, and she smiles at Bernadette.

Bernadette prays her rosary. The Lady has a
rosary, too, and passes the beads through her fingers
as Bernadette prays. Then she turns, and walks away into the rock.

When she tells her family what she's seen, her mother is worried,
wondering who this beautiful stranger is and what she wants with Bernadette.
Reluctantly she agrees that Bernadette may go back to The Grotto, but only if
Toinette and a friend go with her.

Bernadette sees The Lady again, but nobody else does. The Lady asks her to come to The Grotto every day for the next fifteen days and soon everyone in the little town is talking about that strange girl, Bernadette Soubirous, who thinks she is seeing visions. Soon hundreds of people are following her. Some think she's mad or lying, but who can explain the brightness that comes over her face as she prays? Sometimes she appears to listen carefully, sometimes she is joyful, and occasionally she faces the crowd and calls, "We must all repent! Pray for all sinners!"

Today Bernadette is a little afraid as she goes to The Grotto. The crowd is bigger than ever and she knows that they only go because they are inquisitive. Some of them make jokes about her. But when she reaches The Grotto, her beautiful lady is there, smiling a welcome, and Bernadette kneels before her.

"Bernadette," she says, "drink from the fountain and wash in it."

Bernadette is puzzled. There is no fountain here in the cliff – or perhaps there is, and it's hidden, and The Lady wants her to find it? She scrabbles in the earth, scraping and digging with her fingers in the gravel as the hard earth turns wet and muddy on her hands, not noticing the nervous laughter of the crowd. Yes, there's a little pool of water!

She drinks from her hands and washes her face, as The Lady said.

The crowd lean closer to watch her, but they are either laughing or pulling faces of disgust. They can't hear or see The Lady; they only see that lump of a girl putting mud in her mouth and rubbing it into her face. "That's disgusting. Tell the Soubirous family to take her home and keep her there." But when they look again, there is a trickle of water springing up from the ground. The next day, water is spilling over the rocks. An injured girl dips her arm in it and at once she is healed.

After fifteen days, The Lady appears again to Bernadette, and Bernadette asks her name. Later, the priest asks her what The Lady said.

"She said, 'I am the Immaculate Conception,'" says Bernadette.

Bernadette doesn't know that this is a name for Mary, the Mother of Jesus. She only knows that she saw her Beautiful Lady, and her life was transformed, and that the spring still flows down the rocks bringing healing and blessing, again and again. It still does.

*Bernadette saw The Lady for the last time on 16 July 1858. She became a nun with the Sisters of Charity, staying there for the rest of her life. She developed a tubercular swelling in her knee and died on 16 April 1879 at the age of thirty-five.*

*Lourdes is now one of the most famous and popular pilgrim sites in the world. Worship and healing still take place at The Grotto.*

# Padre Pio:
# Saint Pio of Pietrelcina

MAY IS KNOWN by Catholics as Mary's Month, and in May 1887 Francesco Forgione was born in the Italian village of Pietrelcina. All his life he had a great love for Mary, and he later became famous as Padre Pio.

There seem to be some people, very few, who can see and hear things other people can't. They don't choose to be that way – they don't work at it. It's something they're simply born with, and Padre Pio was one of those rare people. From the age of five he experienced visions of Jesus, Mary, and angels and heard them speak to him, but he heard and saw devils, too, which were terrifying. His family were devout Catholics who attended Mass every day. Other boys played at being soldiers or explorers; little Francesco used to play at going to church and singing hymns, and at ten years old he said that he wanted to be "a friar – with a beard!".

After years of study he became a novice in an order of capuchin friars, taking the name "Pio". The plan was that he would become a priest, but it looked as if he wouldn't live long enough to be ordained. He became desperately ill,

suffering terrible migraines and unable to eat or sleep. Evil spirits appeared to him and tormented him. Finally he was sent home to the care of his family. He recovered enough to be ordained a priest in 1910, and it was about that time that he first experienced severe pain in his hands and feet.

He was sent to serve at a mountain village, San Giovanni Rotondo, and soon this remote place became very popular. People who had made their confession to Padre Pio felt that he thoroughly understood them, as if he could see into their minds and hearts, and visitors journeyed long distances to make their confessions to him. The pain in his hands and feet was something he rarely mentioned, except to his own confessor, but the day came when he could no longer keep it secret.

In August 1918, he saw a vision of an angel carrying a sharp lance, then felt a piercing pain in his side. Six weeks later, while praying after Mass, he felt a sense of deep, sweet peace, broken by dazzling light and a startling vision of Jesus, whose hands and feet were bleeding. At that moment, Padre Pio's own hands and feet began to bleed. He was left with "the stigmata", five wounds exactly the same as those of the crucified Jesus Christ.

For the rest of his life Padre

Pio carried the stigmata in his hands, feet, and side. They bled every day and never healed, but never became infected either.

"Suffering is my daily bread," he once said. "I suffer when I do not suffer." He saw his pain as a gift that he could offer to God in prayer, but he was embarrassed about his wounds being visible. Humility was important to him, and he would rather have suffered in secret. "I want to be a friar who prays," he would say, or, "a friar who loves," and prayer was the greatest part of his life.

There are stories of miracles associated with Padre Pio including "bilocation", which means being in two places at the same time! When praying with another friar one night, he suddenly found himself in an elegant house. The man who lived there was on his deathbed while his wife was giving birth to a daughter. The Virgin Mary appeared to Padre Pio, telling him that one day the little girl would seek his help; then the vision faded and Padre Pio found himself back in the chapel. Eighteen years later the girl came to seek his guidance, and he became like a godfather to her.

The commands of Jesus to "love God and your neighbour" were central to his life. As well as his life of prayer, he established a hospital, "The House for the Relief of Suffering", that offered medical care as well as prayer and spiritual support.

At times the Church became suspicious of Padre Pio and limited the work he was allowed to do. He accepted this with humility and patience. "Pray, wait, and don't worry," he would say. "Worrying is useless," and, "Prayer is the best weapon we have; it is the key to the heart of God. You should speak to Jesus, not only with your lips but with your heart."

*Throughout his life Padre Pio had visions of Jesus, Mary, and the angels, but also struggled against the demons that appeared to him. He died, deeply loved, at the age of eighty-one in 1968 and was declared a saint in 2002.*

# Saint Josephine Bakhita

*B*AKHITA. They called her "Bakhita".

It meant "lucky", "fortunate". Why should they call her that? She wasn't lucky when the men came.

In those days, she was not "Bakhita". She had another name, the name that her friends called her when they played in the African sunshine of their village in Darfur, the name that her mother called her when it was time to come in and sit at the table with her family, eating rich dark stew and drinking fresh milk. They called her…

… No, she could not remember what her name was in those days. Horror had wiped it out.

She was about eight years old when the slave traders came and caught her. Day after day, mile after mile, she had walked barefoot until she no longer knew what day it was or where she was. She was sold as a slave and forced to convert to Islam, though she didn't understand anything about it.

Her first owners were kind to her until the day she dropped something by accident. The older son of the family flew into a furious rage, beating, kicking, and whipping her so violently that for the next month she could hardly get up,

let alone walk. Over the next six years in Sudan she was sold again and again and finally bought by a Turkish army officer whose wife and mother beat her every day. She was only Bakhita, their property, worth no more than pots and kettles. Her owner could sell her whenever he wanted to. And he did, because he was returning home and selling his slaves. Fourteen-year-old Bakhita was bought again, this time by an Italian diplomat, Callisto Legnani, who worked abroad for the Italian government.

For the first time since she had been captured, Bakhita was treated kindly. The Legnani family were good to her. Two years later, when they had to go home to Italy, Bakhita begged them to take her with them. The Legnanis agreed, but she wasn't with them for long. In Genoa they met up with old friends, Signor and Signora Michieli, and gave Bakhita to them as a present. The Michielis liked her, and for years she lived in their villa near Venice as nanny to their little girl, Mimmina.

"Bakhita, we're to move again," announced Signora Michieli one morning. "We're selling this house and buying a hotel in Sudan, so we're going back there."

What did Bakhita want? Nobody asked her. The Michielis prepared to go back to Sudan and get their new hotel ready.

"Meanwhile," said Signora Michieli, "you will stay here with Mimmina until we're ready to move in. This house has been sold, but you can stay with the nuns at the Canossian Convent in Venice. We'll come and collect you when we're ready."

So Bakhita was taken to the convent with little Mimmina holding her hand. For the first time she stepped through the doors of the Canossian Convent into the care of the welcoming sisters. Months later, when Signora Michieli came

for her, she refused to leave.

"But Bakhita!" cried Signora Michieli, "How can you do this? You've always been good — you've always done as I told you! You have to come with us! It isn't up to you!"

But Bakhita had found her home, and she knew it. All her life she had wondered about who made the world with all its beauty. In the convent the nuns had told her about God the Creator, and his great love for her. She had learned about Jesus Christ and the gospel had settled in her heart. She wanted more. She wanted to stay and become a nun, and the nuns were happy to have her.

Signora Michieli was furious. She would force Bakhita to come with her if she had to. The nuns went to court to ask a judge for a verdict.

On 29 November 1889, a judge ruled that slavery was illegal and Bakhita was a free woman, old enough to make her own decisions. She'd never been free to make a decision before, but she knew what she wanted to do. She stayed with the Canossian Sisters and was baptized.

*Josephine Margaret Fortunata!* She never remembered her long-ago name, but this was her new name for her new life. In December 1896 she took her final

vows. *Sister Josephine Margaret Fortunata.* She had found her name, her home, her God, her happiness.

For the rest of her life she lived mostly in a convent in Schio, northern Italy, working sometimes as a cook, looking after the chapel, or being the doorkeeper, but she also helped young nuns preparing to work in Africa. Nobody could teach them better, and she longed for the people of Sudan to learn about Jesus Christ. "Her mind was always on God, and her heart in Africa," somebody said.

With her new freedom, she didn't shut herself away in the convent. As the doorkeeper she met the local people and they loved her, especially the children. She had a kind, calm personality, a deep gentle voice, a radiant smile, and a deep love for Jesus and his mother Mary ("Our Lady") and all people. She had a new name now – people called her "black mother". When the Second World War broke out and bombs fell on Schio, the people of the little town felt safe simply because she was there.

*The ill treatment of Josephine Bakhita's slave years had damaged her health and for her last years she was often in pain and needed a wheelchair, but was always cheerful and thankful. She died on 8 February 1947 saying, "I am so happy – Our Lady!" and fifty-three years later Pope John Paul II declared her "Saint Josephine Bakhita".*